Cyberspace Survival Guide

Avoiding Online
HOAXES

By Therese M. Shea

 Gareth Stevens
Publishing

Please visit our website, www.garethstevens.com. For a free color catalog of all our high-quality books, call toll free 1-800-542-2595 or fax 1-877-542-2596.

Library of Congress Cataloging-in-Publication Data

Shea, Therese.
 Avoiding online hoaxes / Therese M. Shea.
    p. cm. — (Cyberspace survival guide)
 Includes index.
 ISBN 978-1-4339-7208-9 (pbk.)
 ISBN978-1-4339-7209-6 (6-pack)
 ISBN 978-1-4339-7207-2 (library binding)
 1. Computer fraud—Juvenile literature. 2. Computer crimes—Juvenile literature. I. Title.
 HV6773.15.C56S54 2013
 613.6—dc23

                                2012007443

First Edition

Published in 2013 by
Gareth Stevens Publishing
111 East 14th Street, Suite 349
New York, NY 10003

Copyright © 2013 Gareth Stevens Publishing

Designer: Katelyn E. Reynolds
Editor: Therese M. Shea

Photo credits: Cover, p. 1 Piti Tan/Shutterstock.com; cover, pp. 1, 3–24 (background) Gala/ Shutterstock.com; cover, pp. 1, 3–24 (grunge banner; cursor graphics; search box graphic) Amgun/ Shutterstock.com; pp. 4, 5, 6, 13, 14, 18, 20 (tablet image) iStockphoto/Thinkstock.com; p. 7 Mike Clarke/AFP/Getty Images; p. 8 1000 Words/Shutterstock.com; p. 9 Sion Touhig/Getty Images; p. 11 Philippe Huguen/AFP/Getty Images; p. 17 Carlos A. Oliveras/Shutterstock.com; p. 19 (TrustedBank email) Andrew Levine/Wikipedia.com; p. 19 (laptop image) Jupiterimages/Brand X Pictures/Thinkstock.com; p. 20 (African Sting email) Matanya/Wikipedia.com; p. 23 Library of Congress, Prints & Photographs Division, photograph by Carol M. Highsmith [reproduction number LC-HS543-207]; p. 24 Hemera/Thinkstock.com; p. 25 Daniel Acker/Bloomberg via Getty Images; p. 26 pzAxe/Shutterstock.com; p. 27 Zero Creatives/Cultura/Getty Images; p. 28 waynehowes/Shutterstock.com.

Printed in the United States of America

CPSIA compliance information: Batch #CS12GS: For further information contact Gareth Stevens, New York, New York at 1-800-542-2595.

CONTENTS

Q Words in the glossary appear in **bold** type the first time they are used in the text.

Hoaxes AND SPAM

Have you ever received an e-mail and not known who the sender was? This happens to some people many times a day. In recent years, it's almost impossible to keep "junk" from leaking into our e-mail accounts. Spam e-mails are one kind of junk e-mail. Spam is the name for unrequested messages from businesses or organizations that are sent to many e-mail addresses at once.

Another kind of junk e-mail is masked as important **information**. It may even come from your friends! This is hoax e-mail. A hoax is any act meant to trick someone into believing something that isn't true.

How did spam e-mails get their name? A British TV show called *Monty Python's Flying Circus* featured a funny story about a restaurant that served the meat product Spam. The word "spam" was repeated many, many times. People who get a lot of repeating e-mails get very annoyed at spam, just like the people in the show!

It's often easy to spot spam e-mails. Hoaxes can be trickier.

E-mail FILTERS

Most e-mail services have **filters** that check incoming e-mails and "guess" which pieces are spam. These e-mails are placed in a spam—or junk—folder. There, users can examine them and decide their worth. You may also be able to change the settings in your account to block certain addresses.

However, hoax e-mails are often sent to you by people you know because they may believe the hoax. This means that your e-mail service probably won't block the e-mail because it's coming from an approved address. This also means you need to know how to spot a hoax e-mail.

Spam

Spam

Spam

Spam

Spam

Spam

Spam

Did you ever open an e-mail and see a bunch of words that didn't make sense? There was probably a link to a website, too. This is a kind of spam. Spammers put those words in the e-mail so that antispam programs won't catch their messages. They also misspell names of products they're selling so the programs won't identify their purpose.

Computer users can save themselves time—and sometimes money—by not sending e-mail hoaxes to others. Spam is harder to avoid.

Many Kinds, MANY PLACES

There are many kinds of e-mail hoaxes. For example, someone may send an e-mail containing a photo that has been changed using computer programs, such as a picture of a three-headed cat. The photo was made to trick someone into thinking the three-headed cat exists. Most people know a hoax like this is false. However, there are other e-mail hoaxes that seem true.

Common hoaxes involve charities, sick children, computer **viruses**, money, **chain letters**, warnings, **petitions**, and advice—and none of it's true! Hoaxes aren't just in e-mail either. They're anywhere on the Internet where people share information, such as **blogs**, Facebook, and Twitter.

Hoax or Joke?

Some hoax e-mails are jokes. They poke fun at other hoaxes. For example, one joke hoax warns about a computer virus that can spread through electrical lines. It suggests people no longer use computers, electricity, or even batteries! Usually, joke hoaxes are "over the top," so it's easy to see that the sender was joking.

BBC NEWS

You are in: World: Europe
Wednesday, 13 June, 2001, 10:57 GMT 10:57 UK

Britney Spears killed in crash

Front Page
World

Africa
Americas
Asia-Pacific
Europe
Middle East

Some hoaxes spread rumors or even lies, such as this story that singer Britney Spears had been killed in a car crash. Many news agencies believed it!

Why Do People CREATE HOAXES?

Why do people create hoaxes? They may want to see how far e-mails spread or how many e-mail addresses they can collect. Some hoaxes have been bouncing from e-mail inbox to e-mail inbox for years. A few warnings about fake computer viruses have been around since the early 1990s. This means people have been forwarding the same hoax for more than 20 years!

Some people want to become famous for their hoaxes. Other hoaxes start out as jokes for a group of friends but are forwarded to other people. Still other people use hoaxes to make money by tricking people. Many people write hoaxes just because they can!

🔍 The E-Card Hoax

One famous hoax, first appearing in 2000, warned of a virus contained in e-mails with the subject "Virtual Card for You." The e-mail claimed that people who clicked on a link in an e-mail to receive an e-card would transfer a virus into their computer. The virus would then erase the computer's memory. However, there was no such virus.

People have many reasons for creating e-mail hoaxes. Unfortunately, once a hoax starts, it can be hard to stop.

Spotting A HOAX

Many hoax e-mails share features. Here are some hints that an e-mail is a hoax:

1. The e-mail tells you to forward it to more people. Hoax writers want their message to spread, so they tell the receiver to forward it. If everyone who receives a message sends it to more people, the message spreads widely and quickly.

Hoax creators often use people's feelings to convince them to forward the e-mail. For example, they may try to make you feel scared about a certain danger. You'll read the e-mail and then forward the message so your friends will know about the danger, too.

Some hoaxes, such as chain letters, try to convince the receiver to forward them to a certain number of people. In exchange, they promise the sender will receive a prize, good luck, or something else. They may also try to scare the receiver by saying they'll get bad luck if they don't send it. Just remember, it's only a hoax!

A new virus is circulating!!!!

This information came from Microsoft, and Norton. Please, transmit it to anybody that you know that has access to the Internet.

You may receive an e-mail about an offensive Powerpoint Presentation, entitled "Life is beautiful.pps".

If you get it, DO NOT OPEN THE FILE UNDER ANY CIRCUMSTANCE and delete it immediately.

If you open that file a message will appear on your screen, "Now it is late, your life is no longer beautiful" after that you'll lose EVERYTHING IN YOUR PC and the person who sent it will have access to your name, e-mail address, and password.

It is a new virus started to run Saturday night.

We need TO DO ALL THAT is POSSIBLE TO DETAIN THAT VIRUS.

UOL already confirmed its danger and antivirus software cannot destroyed it.

The Virus was created by a hacker that denominates himself as the owner of Microsoft in justice!

Because of this it comes disguised with a .PPS extension. He fights in justice life and wants to destroy PCs domestic, and fight against Microsoft in justice! by the patent of the Windows-XP.

SEND THIS E-MAIL TO ALL YOUR FRIENDS

This hoax e-mail tells the receiver to "send this e-mail to all your friends."

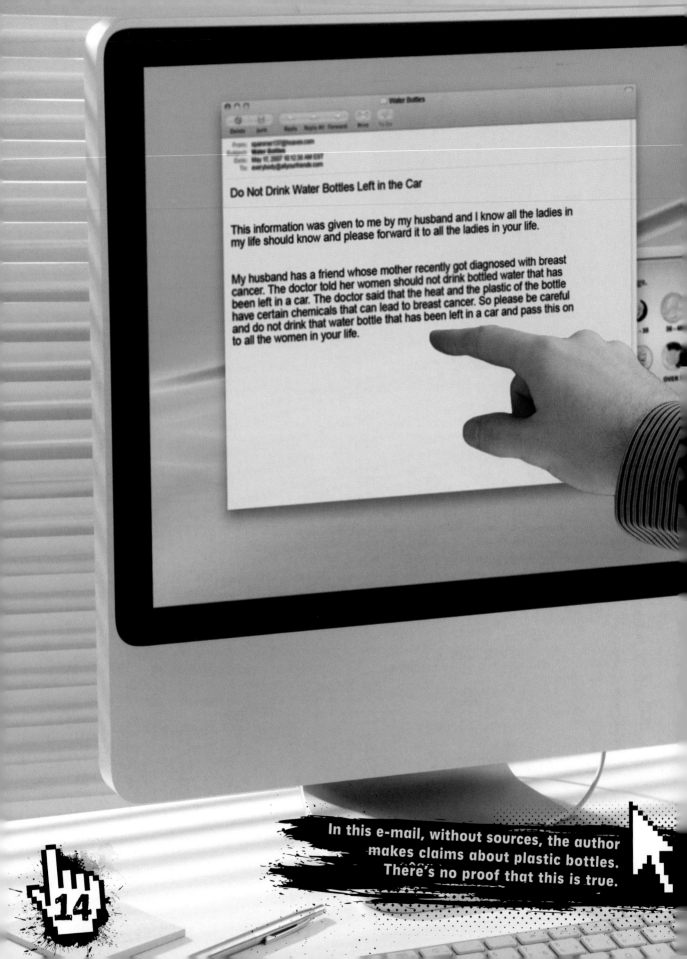

Do Not Drink Water Bottles Left in the Car

This information was given to me by my husband and I know all the ladies in my life should know and please forward it to all the ladies in your life.

My husband has a friend whose mother recently got diagnosed with breast cancer. The doctor told her women should not drink bottled water that has been left in a car. The doctor said that the heat and the plastic of the bottle have certain chemicals that can lead to breast cancer. So please be careful and do not drink that water bottle that has been left in a car and pass this on to all the women in your life.

In this e-mail, without sources, the author makes claims about plastic bottles. There's no proof that this is true.

2. There are no sources to back up the claims in the e-mail.

E-mails that claim a company is giving away a prize or that give health advice are often hoaxes. If they were factual, they'd provide trustworthy sources to back up their claims. A direct link to a website should prove the information is true. The e-mail may also give the name of an organization so someone can check the facts.

Did the person who sent the e-mail write it? If not, did the person who wrote the e-mail sign their name?

There's no way of telling how truthful the original sender is if you don't know who they are.

🔍 Fake Sources

Some hoax e-mails seem trustworthy. They may give the name of a doctor or medical journal, for example. However, sometimes these people or publications don't exist. They're included to persuade people to believe the message. So how can you tell? Do the research or check with online organizations that do the checking for you.

3. The e-mail uses "exciting" punctuation and language.

Beware of exclamation points! Hoax e-mails often have a lot of exclamation points. The writer is trying to excite you about the contents of the message. They may also use all capital letters for the same effect. For example, compare these two sentences:

Act now or you may miss a great chance to get rich.

Act NOW or you may miss a GREAT CHANCE to get RICH!!

Which sentence makes you feel more excited? Most people would say the second. The writer also uses words such as "now" and "rich" to get you to act quickly.

🔍 A Sick Child Hoax

A 2011 hoax on Facebook asked users to post a story about a child sick with cancer. It promised that Facebook would give money to a charity every time someone "shared" the story on their page. The hoax didn't provide any links to Facebook proving it was true. In fact, the whole story was made up. The hoax writer knew that people feel sorry for sick children and act on that feeling.

From:

spammer732@

To:

johnsmith@them

ject:

MONEY!!!!!!!!!!!!!!!!!!!!

10 ▼

If spammers used e-mail addresses like this one, they'd be easier to spot. Unfortunately, they're usually much trickier.

17

PHISHING

Phishing is the act of using e-mail to get personal information for a bad purpose. Phishing hoaxes are harmful **scams**. The sender may ask you to reply to an e-mail with your information, or the sender may provide a link to a site that looks **authentic**. The fake site can look just like a bank or store website. Users give their bank account numbers or credit card information to these sites.

So how do you protect yourself from phishing? Never respond to an e-mail by providing personal information. Also, never click on a link within a phishing e-mail. Type addresses into the address bar of the Internet **browser**.

Phishing gets its name from the sport of fishing. Fishermen put bait on a hook for a fish to nibble on. When the fish bites, the fisherman has it on the hook and can reel it in. Phishers use bait such as asking for credit card information. Once the user "bites," phishers can use this information to steal money.

TrustedBank™

Dear valued customer of TrustedBank,

We have recieved notice that you have recently attempted to withdraw the following amount from your checking account while in another country: $135.25.

If this information is not correct, someone unknown may have access to your account. As a safety measure, please visit our website via the link below to verify your personal information:

http://www.trustedbank.com/general/custverifyinfo.asp

Once you have done this, our fraud department will work to resolve this discrepency. We are happy you have chosen us to do business with.

Thank you,
TrustedBank

Member FDIC © 2005 TrustedBank, Inc

A "phisher" may use an e-mail address that looks like a business e-mail, but that doesn't mean it's not a scam.

I am contacting you in respect of a family treasure of Gold deposited in my name

From: **becky** (becky_time5001@rediffmail.com)   Mark as safe | Mark as unsafe

⚠ You may not know this sender. Mark as safe. Mark as unsafe

Sent: Wed 8/15/07 11:59 AM
To: becky_time5001@rediffmail.com

i am Becky Ofori a Ghanian from Ashanti region Kumasi, Ghana ...
treasure of Gold deposited in my name by my late father who was ... and Diamond mer...
As a well known business man,and a stong politician ,my father was brutally murdered d...
J.J. Rawlings the ex- president of the federal republic of Ghana , as he was accused of m...
public against the government of the day. Been a poligamous home , and my mother be...
loving wife was abandoned after the death of my father by members of his family . As a...
mother carefull and stiff handling of my fathers estate while he was alive. We were kic...
benefitting from any of my fathers shared estate. My mum w... humiliated and i and m...
left at the mercy of my elder brothers,
    Right now we are passing through great difficulties ar...
father while he was alive, deposited a consignment of ...
outfit in my country.We have made all inquiry to confi...
and i have decided to sell this consignment of gold to a...
proceeds to put our lives on course again by leaving Afri...
    I want you to come to Ghana and see for yourself what i a...
the sale overseas .We are prepared to go into any agreement for perc...
help , and we are very much prepared to part with 20% of the sales mon...
    On the contrary, if you are a potential buyer ,then a fresh agreement wou...
transaction,
    I am looking forward to hear from you in this respect as soon as you receive th...

One type of phishing hoax is the Nigerian scam. Its name stems from the African country of Nigeria, from which many of the e-mails come. The sender asks for help in a matter involving thousands or even millions of dollars. They write that some of the money will be given to anyone who helps them. Another version of the scam claims that someone has won the lottery. The sender asks for bank information so that the money can be put into an account.

Of course, the money is never sent. In fact, millions of dollars have been stolen from people's accounts because of the Nigerian scam.

🔍 Something for Nothing

The Nigerian scam and similar hoaxes can all be grouped as "something for nothing" scams. That is, someone promises to give something away for next to nothing. Remember, anything that seems too good to be true usually is. People who have lost money to phishers in other countries will probably never get it back.

21

If you come across a scam e-mail asking for personal information, you should first show your parents. They can then forward the e-mail to the proper authority. If the sender pretends to be from a business, the real business can take action to warn others.

Government agencies also want to know about money scams. Some of these agencies include the Internet Crime Complaint Center (www.ic3.gov/complaint/), the Federal Trade Commission (spam@uce.gov), and your state attorney general's office. They can often track down the source of the scam and put a stop to it, or they can issue a general warning.

🔍 Be Safe on the Web!

Even if you don't have a bank account, you should never give any information about yourself—such as how old you are or where you live—to a stranger on the Internet. People can and have pretended to be other people through e-mail and through sites such as Facebook. You can never be sure who someone on the Internet really is.

FEDERAL TRADE
COMMISSION

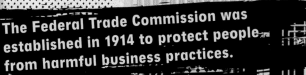

The Federal Trade Commission was established in 1914 to protect people from harmful business practices.

Spiders ON THE WEB

So how do scammers and phishers get an e-mail address in the first place? Any e-mail address on a public Internet site is at risk of receiving spam, hoaxes, and scams. A program called a spider is made to search the Internet for information.

Spiders can be helpful. Some collect data for search engines, such as Google. But scammers can use "spyware" spiders to search for e-mail addresses. If your address is on a site, a spider may grab it for phishing purposes. When the phishing scam is sent out, it goes to many, many addresses. If just one person falls for it, the scammer wins.

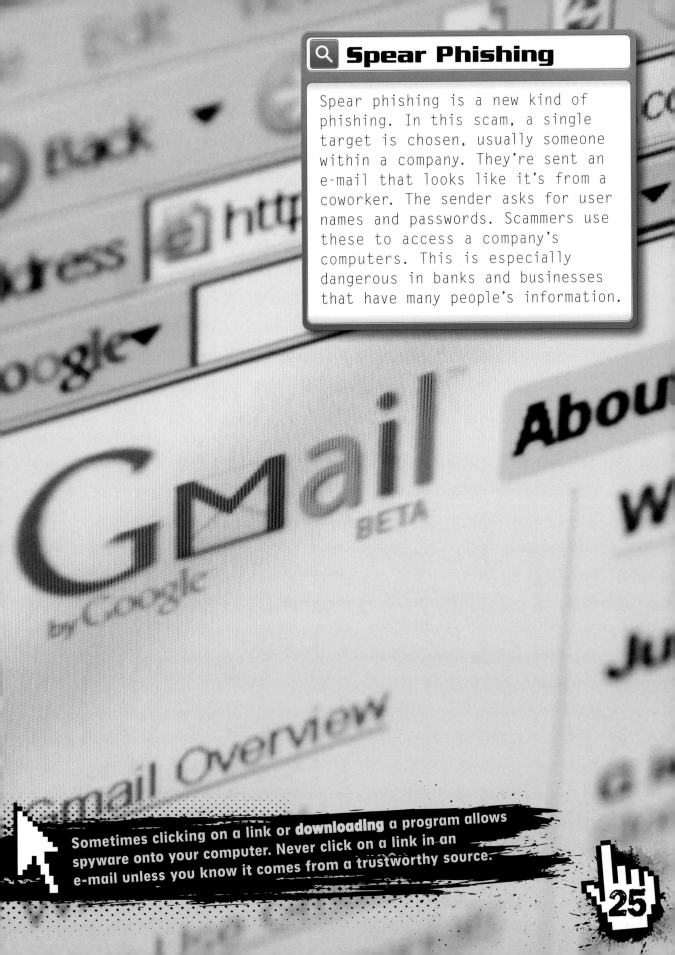

Spear Phishing

Spear phishing is a new kind of phishing. In this scam, a single target is chosen, usually someone within a company. They're sent an e-mail that looks like it's from a coworker. The sender asks for user names and passwords. Scammers use these to access a company's computers. This is especially dangerous in banks and businesses that have many people's information.

Sometimes clicking on a link or **downloading** a program allows spyware onto your computer. Never click on a link in an e-mail unless you know it comes from a trustworthy source.

You Can Fight HOAXES!

Once you realize a message is a hoax, you have several choices of how to act. First, do nothing. Don't send it on to others. Use the websites listed in this book to see if the hoax or scam has been reported already.

You can respond to the person who sent it to you, but only if you know them. Perhaps telling them it's a hoax will make them think twice about forwarding a similar e-mail. But if the e-mail is a scam to get money or personal information that may put someone in danger, you should tell an adult so they can take action.

🔍 Growing Numbers

How quickly can a hoax spread? If just one person sends a hoax to 10 friends who each send it to 10 friends, it's in 100 inboxes. If those 100 people send it on to 10 people each, the hoax is now in 1,000 inboxes. Keep multiplying to find out just how quickly a message spreads on the Internet!

By becoming smart about e-mail hoaxes, people can protect themselves, their computers, and other people.

In recent years, sites such as Twitter and Facebook have been invaded by hoaxes. What's the big deal about hoaxes? They may give unhealthy advice to people, which can be harmful. They may tell people false ideas about businesses and organizations. They may cause people to worry about things such as computer viruses that don't even exist. They may lead to people losing money. Finally, they're simply a waste of time in many ways.

You can research facts for yourself rather than believing everything you read on the Internet. And you can do other people a favor by not forwarding hoaxes that may cause harm for years to come.

ask that the message be forwarded on to many other people

promise "something for nothing"

ask for personal information

Features of Hoaxes

include "over the top" claims

don't include trustworthy sources of information

use language and punctuation to excite or scare

GLOSSARY

authentic: true and trustworthy

blog: an online journal. Short for "web log."

browser: a computer program that allows a user to get on the Internet and look at information

chain letter: a letter sent to a number of people, each of whom is asked to send it to a certain number of people

download: to transfer or copy files from one computer to another, or from the Internet to a computer

filter: a tool that allows some items to pass and blocks others

information: knowledge or facts

petition: a written request signed by many people demanding an action

scam: a trick for making money

virus: a computer program that is usually hidden and makes copies of itself that it puts into other programs, causing harm

For More INFORMATION

Books

Bailey, Diane. *Cyber Ethics*. New York, NY: Rosen Central, 2008.

Hunter, Nick. *Internet Safety*. Chicago, IL: Heinemann Library, 2012.

Websites

The Case of the Cyber Criminal
onguardonline.gov/media/game-0013-case-cyber-criminal
Play a game while answering questions about cyber crimes.

FBI: New E-Scams and Warnings
www.fbi.gov/scams-safety/e-scams
Find out about the newest scams, and read tips about how to keep from getting fooled.

Internet Fraud
www.fraud.org/internet/intinfo.htm
Read about scams on the Internet on the site for the National Internet Fraud Watch Information Center.

INDEX